A DEVIL INSIDE

BY DAVID LINDSAY-ABAIRE

★

★

DRAMATISTS
PLAY SERVICE
INC.

A Devil Inside was produced by Soho Rep (Julian Webber, Artistic Director) in New York City on January 8, 1997. It was directed by Julian Webber; the set design was by Molly Hughes; the lighting design was by Adam Silverman; the sound design was by John Kilgore; the costume design was by Anne Lammel; and the production stage manager was Gretchen Knowlton. The cast was as follows:

GENE .... Bill Dawes
MRS. SLATER .... Marylouise Burke
CARL .... Larry Block
CAITLIN .... Heather Goldenhersh
BRAD .... John McAdams
LILY .... Pamela Nyberg

CHARACTERS

GENE is twenty-one, boyish and a little naive. Even in his most profound moments of understanding, he's still in the dark.

MRS. SLATER is in her fifties. She's tough as nails and has experienced loads of tragedy in her life, but still she perseveres. She runs a laundromat.

CARL is a Russian Literature professor in his early fifties, tormented by his relentless thoughts and nightmares.

CAITLIN is barely twenty. She's a wide-eyed romantic, fiery and impetuous. Despite her fits of toughness, she is as young as Gene is boyish.

BRAD is in his mid-thirties, a ridiculously plain man who longs for something more than the appliance repair shop that he runs.

LILY is in her late thirties. She's a physically fit artist with secrets of her own. She's intriguing and a bit of a mystery.

SET

The set, with its numerous locations, should be simple and representational. There should be as few set changes as possible. Nothing should stop the flow of the play.

A DEVIL INSIDE

ACT ONE

Scene 1

Lights up on a rundown laundromat. We hear washers and dryers running. There's a sign posted that says "Not Responsible for Lost or Stolen Items." Mrs. Slater is hanging a homemade "Happy Birthday" banner. She is middle-aged and wears a huge belt crisscrossing her chest. A scrap of pink blanket is pinned to her sweater. She's like a decorated war hero. We hear her son Gene calling from offstage.

GENE. *(Off.)* Where are my boots? ... Mom? ... I can't find my boots. *(Gene enters. He has overslept. He's twenty-one, half-dressed and late for class.)* Have you seen my boots?
MRS. SLATER. Happy Birthday, sweetheart.
GENE. Thanks. Do you know where my boots are?
MRS. SLATER. No, I don't. But I made you this banner. Want me to sing to you?
GENE. I'm late, Mom.
MRS. SLATER. That's because you sleep too much. Just like your Dad. Boy could he sleep. *(Gene rummages through various laundry baskets for something to wear.)* Gene, there's something I have to tell you.
GENE. *(Looking through laundry carts.)* Well hurry it up, I gotta go.
MRS. SLATER. All right then ... *(Looks around to make sure no one's listening, then:)* Son ... your father was murdered. He was stabbed in the back and his feet were lopped off and thrown into

5

a drainage ditch.

GENE. *(Beat.)* Okay. Was that it?

MRS. SLATER. He was a fat man, but he was wonderful, and someone murdered him.

GENE. No sign of those boots then?

MRS. SLATER. Someone took the life of a lovely fat man.

GENE. Mom?

MRS. SLATER. Yes?

GENE. My father died of a heart attack.

MRS. SLATER. I knew you'd take this hard.

GENE. *(Pulls plaid shirt from laundry cart and puts it on.)* Who left this?

MRS. SLATER. Mrs. Pitooly. But you can't wear other people's clothes. That's a very dirty thing to do. *(But Gene has already put it on.)* Did you hear what I said? About your father?

GENE. Yes, I did. I have Russian Lit until noon. There's a big detergent delivery this morning. Make sure the guy carries it in himself. You're obviously not feeling well.

MRS. SLATER. Are you kidding me? I feel like a million bucks!

GENE. I'm gonna talk to Doctor Krebbs about your pills. You look flushed.

MRS. SLATER. You don't believe me.

GENE. It's just the heat from the dryers again. Remember that time you saw elves hiding in the light fixtures? Same thing.

MRS. SLATER. It's not the same thing!

GENE. Open the doors, air this place out.

MRS. SLATER. You gotta listen to me, Gene. I just said it was a heart attack because I didn't want you to have bad dreams. I've been waiting fourteen years to tell you the truth. You're twenty-one today. You're a man now. I want you to avenge your father's death.

GENE. I can't avenge heart failure, Mama. *(The sound of dogs barking outside.)*

MRS. SLATER. Those damn dogs. The garbage collectors are on strike and Schultzy puts bags of rotten meat on the sidewalks. *(Runs to the window and bangs on it.)* Get out of here, you filthy mutts! I'll string you up! *(Goes to desk and grabs flyers.)* I had some flyers made to drum up some business. Here, pass them out to people on the street.

GENE. *(Pulling on socks.)* All right.

MRS. SLATER. *(Pulls photo from pocket.)* Wasn't he handsome? Sure, he weighed 416 pounds, but he wasn't happy that way. He read that he could burn off two pounds if he walked three miles. So he was gonna walk until he reached his ideal weight. I packed his clothes. His big white briefs. I wrote his name inside the waistband, just like he was going to camp. And I packed a silk scarf, so he could think of me. And he walked!

GENE. Until his heart exploded in the Pennsylvania Poconos.

MRS. SLATER. His heart didn't explode! Someone whacked him in the back with an ax and cut off his feet! It was one of those serial people. They found another foot up in the hills, you know. A foot without a body!

GENE. Mama —

MRS. SLATER. He never did anything to anyone. You can't kill an innocent man. You have no place in this world if you do something like that. *(Gene has opened a dryer and found his boots.)*

GENE. Look what I found.

MRS. SLATER. I polished them for you.

GENE. You were hiding them.

MRS. SLATER. For fourteen years I planned this day. Your birthday. It had to be you, Gene. Sons avenge fathers. That's how it is in families. Otherwise, I'd do it myself. But I've been saving, Gene. Rolls and rolls of quarters. So when this is all over, we can buy a house in the Hamptons. You can find a wife and give me grandchildren. Strong grandchildren. You'll cleanse the family, Gene.

GENE. I have to go.

MRS. SLATER. Then go! Go to school! But remember who paid to send you to that college!

GENE. I make money.

MRS. SLATER. Pocket change! Look at my hands. Have you worked this hard? The sweat that has dripped off of me over the years could flood the city. That and my tears. I've never asked you for anything.

GENE. *(Heading to door.)* Bye, Mama.

MRS. SLATER. You have to find the truth. It's what your father would want. *(Calling after him.)* Avenge him, Gene! Avenge your footless father! *(Blackout.)*

7

Scene 2

Subway car. Gene is staring at Caitlin. Caitlin is reading. Gene finally gets up enough courage to speak to her.

GENE. You're Caitlin, right? *(Caitlin looks up from her book.)* I'm Gene Slater.
CAITLIN. Do I know you?
GENE. I'm in your Russian Lit lecture.
CAITLIN. You look very familiar.
GENE. I sit in the back row.
CAITLIN. More familiar than that. Eerily familiar.
GENE. I see you on the train a lot.
CAITLIN. You should say hello.
GENE. Well ... you're usually reading and ... I don't wanna bother you.
CAITLIN. But today you got brave. *(Beat.)* It's creepy how familiar you are to me.
GENE. I stare at you in class, maybe you've seen me.
CAITLIN. Do you like my shoes?
GENE. Uh ... yeah. They're nice.
CAITLIN. Do they make me look taller? More imposing?
GENE. Sure.
CAITLIN. I just bought them. I like the way they make me feel. You stare at me?
GENE. Sometimes.
CAITLIN. You shouldn't do that. It's rude. *(Beat.)* Do you enjoy the class? I do. I love it. I want to eat the books I love them so much. He's an incredible man. He arouses me.
GENE. Professor Raymonds?
CAITLIN. He's a tormented soul. I love that about him. *(Holds up book.)* This is his new book. *Dostoyevsky's Nightmares.* Literary criticism.
GENE. Sounds dry.

8

CAITLIN. It's not. Can I tell you something?

GENE. All right.

CAITLIN. I've been following him for two weeks. When he goes somewhere, I follow him. I hide and I watch. I'm very discreet. Do you think I'm crazy? Go ahead, say that I am. Tell me I'm a fool to love him. Tell me he's my professor. Tell me he's twice my age, Jerry!

GENE. Gene. My name is Gene.

CAITLIN. He has this little bar where he goes to write in his journal. I sit in there sometimes and just watch him write.

GENE. You watch him write?

CAITLIN. He's awful. He smokes and drinks and swears. He has the weight of his life strapped to his back, dragging behind him like a giant cart filled with cast-iron cannon balls. Just like me. *(Smiles at Gene.)* But you have no idea what I'm talking about. I can see how carefree your life has been. You're a lucky boy, Jerry. Lucky and eerily familiar. *(Lights fade as they ride on.)*

Scene 3

Lecture hall. Professor Carl Raymonds is lecturing about Crime and Punishment.

CARL. I passed a shop today and inside was the dullest looking man I've ever seen, fixing a toaster, and I thought what if I killed him? What if I pulled out a gun and shot this worthless man, and no one saw me do it? Could I get away with it? Would anyone care that he was dead? Would I feel anything having done it? *(Beat.)* Strange thoughts, right? Amusing things to think about. But then I moved on with my day. And you know what? I couldn't get those ideas out of my head. They're like a persistent tune I can't shake. Even now, I'm standing here and I'm supposed to lecture about *Crime and Punishment*, but my head keeps going back to that man in that shop. *(Beat.)* Does that remind you of Raskolnikov? It does me. His obsession with the old woman he wants to murder. His justifying her death because of her worthless place in society and her mistreatment of others. None of us are so far from the murderer that skulks his way through this novel, are we? *(Beat.)* Shall we talk about his dream? A little horse with pitiful eyes is whipped to death by a thug while a child looks on helplessly. What's it mean? Isn't his sister compromising herself into a marriage of convenience? Isn't Dunya the horse? What about the drunk girl, and Sonya and Lizaveta? Aren't they *all* horses with pitiful eyes brutalized by men? *(Beat.)* And what's with St. Petersburg? I know I'm jumping around here, but try to keep up because — St. Petersburg. People leaping off bridges, lunatics in the streets, wild animals, fits, fights. Is this the *actual* city or simply the manifestation of his diseased mind? If he has all these ugly ideas crowding his head, of course the world is gonna look like — He starts hearing people whispering about murder. Everyone seems vile. The streets are wretched. His nightmares are coming to life, aren't they? He's losing control, right? And if he loses control, he becomes the thing he fears most: the whipped horse in his dream! He becomes all of those women! *(Beat.)* So he makes a plan. He says I need to take control. I need to get this crap out of my head! I'm not a victim! I'm not a horse! I'm not a woman! He says I'm a murderer, a man, a horrible, violent thug with a whip, with a penis that kills! And he crosses a line. His obsessions take over. His dreams become reality, his reality becomes a dream. And he goes there as he planned and he kills that old woman to gain control, but the retarded half-sister shows up and he has to kill her too. Now the control he sought is nowhere to be found. In control and out of control. Dream and reality. Murderer and victim. They're all the same in a dream! They're interchangeable. And if his dreams become his reality, then the rules in his dream-world carry over. You see the futility? You can't make plans in dreams, you can't try to control a nightmare. And *Crime and Punishment*, the book itself, is a horrible nightmare come to life! *(Blackout.)*

10

Scene 4

Appliance repair shop. Brad is repairing an electric carving knife. Lily is drawing in a large sketchpad and eating a protein bar.

BRAD. Do you think I'm plain?

LILY. *(Pause.)* Do I what?

BRAD. Do you think I'm plain?

LILY. How do you mean?

BRAD. I don't know. It just occurred to me that maybe I'm dull. I mean, I don't really do much of anything. Besides take things apart. And no one's ever taken an interest in me it seems, and I just started thinking that maybe I'm a little plain. I don't suppose you'd be here if it weren't for the back room. *(Beat.)* Sometimes I feel like a ghost. But not a scary ghost. The other kind. A nice ghost. One that's there, watching people, but they don't notice him because he's an invisible and benevolent spirit.

LILY. *(Looking up from the sketchpad.)* Hm?

BRAD. Forget it.

LILY. No, I'm sorry. You were saying something about pie?

BRAD. No.

LILY. Oh. I thought you said something about pie.

BRAD. I didn't. I was talking about ghosts.

LILY. Oh. *(Beat.)* You don't *have* any pie, do ya?

BRAD. No.

LILY. That's too bad. I could really go for some pie right now.

BRAD. Well I don't have any.

LILY. Oh well. *(Goes back to sketching.)*

BRAD. *(Pause.)* You like the back room?

LILY. Very much. Thanks for letting me stay there.

BRAD. I'm glad to have the company. Usually I just talk to myself.

LILY. I'll try to not to get in the way. It'll be a couple weeks tops.

BRAD. Stay as long you want. I don't mind. *(Pause.)* So when did you become an artist?

LILY. Brad, you promised.

BRAD. Oh right. Sorry. No questions.

LILY. It's just … a very complicated situation I'm in. I don't wanna get you involved.

BRAD. I wouldn't mind.

LILY. It's better you not know anything about me.

BRAD. *(Beat.)* You're interesting, aren't ya? Mysterious, artistic. I don't do anything.

LILY. Well, it's never too late.

BRAD. That's true. I used to write stories in college.

LILY. Well, there ya go. You should write a story.

BRAD. Or maybe I could learn how to skateboard.

LILY. Either one. Sounds great. Do you have a *Yellow Pages?*

BRAD. Over on the shelf. *(Lily goes to get* Yellow Pages. *She rifles through it while Brad is talking.)* There's this young man at Astor Place who does skateboard tricks. I've always wanted to do something like that.

LILY. *(Nose in* Yellow Pages.*)* Sounds dangerous.

BRAD. He waits until all the lights are red so no traffic's crossing his path and then he comes at us really fast on the skateboard and jumps over eight trash baskets. People love it. Yeah, that's what I wanna do. I wanna jump over trash, instead of fixing it, instead of being buried in it. *(Mrs. Slater walks into store and looks around suspiciously.)*

MRS. SLATER. Ya fix things?

BRAD. That's right.

MRS. SLATER. Good, 'cause this is busted. *(Slams a compass on the counter.)*

BRAD. It's a compass.

MRS. SLATER. Uh huh.

BRAD. It'd be cheaper to just buy another compass, ma'am.

MRS. SLATER. It has to be this one. I want it fixed.

BRAD. I can probably do it by tomorrow.

MRS. SLATER. I hope so. I'm gonna need that compass.

BRAD. I'll do my best.

MRS. SLATER. *(To Lily.)* What are you drawing?

LILY. Who me?

BRAD. She doesn't like questions.

MRS. SLATER. *(Referring to sketch.)* Is that a foot?

BRAD. Yeah, it's mine. She was drawing it. She's obsessed with feet. That's all she draws. She has sculptures of feet. Paintings of feet. Feet. Feet. Everything feet.

LILY. That's not true. I do a lot of things. He doesn't know me very well.

BRAD. She's right. I hardly know her at all. And yet I still let her live in my back room. That's sorta crazy, isn't it?

MRS. SLATER. Just fix my compass. I got things to do.

BRAD. Yes ma'am.

MRS. SLATER. I'll be back tomorrow. *(Exits.)*

LILY. I wish you wouldn't talk about me to other people.

BRAD. You mean the foot thing? I didn't realize it was a secret.

LILY. Everything's a secret, Brad. Everything.

BRAD. I'm sorry. *(Pause.)* I didn't tell her about your hair. You know how it used to be brown but now it's not?

LILY. Yes Brad, my hair used to be brown. What is your point?

BRAD. Just that I didn't tell her *everything*. *(Beat.)* I fixed the electric knife. *(He clicks the electric knife on. It buzzes.)*

LILY. Nice work.

BRAD. Thank you. Hey, you wanna see the walls in my room?

LILY. For what?

BRAD. You might wanna sketch them. I was lying in bed last night, picking shapes out of the patterns on the wallpaper, and I noticed a laughing devil head, and it's everywhere because that's what wallpaper patterns are like. So my room is filled with laughing devil heads and I had to leave because it started scaring me a little. Devil head. Devil head. Devil head. It made me nervous. That's why I slept on this table last night.

LILY. I was wondering about that.

BRAD. Lily … can you just tell me one thing?

LILY. No.

BRAD. What happened to you?

LILY. I said no.

BRAD. I thought you'd get in touch, but you never did.

LILY. I'm here, aren't I?

BRAD. Sure, but fourteen years —

LILY. I need to go get a few things. *(Packs up her sketch pad.)*
BRAD. Oh. At the art store?
LILY. Uh … Yeah.
BRAD. All right. Maybe we can talk later.
LILY. No, I don't think so. *(Exits. Brad takes the compass apart. The phone rings.)*
BRAD. *(Answering phone.)* Brad's Fix-it Shop … Yes, it's ready. There was a problem with the heating coils. I replaced them. *(Carl appears at window, looking in at Brad. He's writing notes in his journal.)* A jukebox? … No, but I could try … Anytime tomorrow. All right, I'll see you then. *(Brad hangs up phone. He looks over and sees Carl, who stares back, then walks off suddenly. Brad runs to the window and looks after him. Lights fade.)*

Scene 5

Laundromat. Gene and Caitlin enter, having just come from class.

CAITLIN. *(Thrilled.)* I'm still trembling. Do you see what he does to me?
GENE. I think he's a freak.
CAITLIN. Yes he is, and I love that about him. All that talk about nightmares makes me giddy. You know, I've been haunted by a peculiar dream since I was this high.
GENE. Is that right?
CAITLIN. *(Suddenly notices.)* This place smells like bleach.
GENE. It's a laundromat.
MRS. SLATER. *(Off.)* Gene, is that you?
GENE. That's my mother. You wanna see freaky —
MRS. SLATER. *(Enters.)* I'm glad you're back. No running this time. *(To Caitlin.)* You there, block the door. *(To Gene.)* I got something to show ya.
GENE. Can't you show me later?

14

MRS. SLATER. *(To Caitlin.)* Who *are* you anyway?

CAITLIN. Caitlin. I'm in Gene's class.

MRS. SLATER. Caitlin, huh? Funny name. What is it, Spanish?

CAITLIN. *(Confused.)* No.

MRS. SLATER. Doesn't matter. This family doesn't have any more secrets. *(Handing her flyers.)* Here, take some flyers. Give them to friends.

GENE. We're gonna study upstairs.

MRS. SLATER. Hey, this ain't a library, you know! *(To Caitlin.)* I said block the door!

GENE. Mom —

MRS. SLATER. Gene, it's your birthday, and I got a gift for ya.

CAITLIN. You didn't tell me it was your birthday. *(Mrs. Slater goes behind desk and pulls out a large gift-wrapped present.)*

MRS. SLATER. This is from me and your Dad. He would want you to have something special. *(Gene unwraps the gift. It's a huge jar. Inside the jar, the amputated feet of Gene's father are floating in formaldehyde.)* Whaddaya think of that?

GENE. *(Looks, then realizes what they are.)* Sweet Jesus!

MRS. SLATER. I know it's shocking, but you're a man now.

CAITLIN. What the hell is that?

MRS. SLATER. Gene doesn't believe that his father's feet were chopped off.

GENE. Are those real?

MRS. SLATER. Where am I gonna get a pair of fake feet?

CAITLIN. Those are feet?

GENE. You've kept my father's feet in a jar?

MRS. SLATER. It's formaldehyde. I kept them behind the furnace.

GENE. I don't *believe* this.

MRS. SLATER. *(To Caitlin.)* He's in denial. *(To Gene.)* But you have to believe it, Gene, it's your birthday. I wouldn't lie on a day like this.

CAITLIN. They're so big.

MRS. SLATER. For the sake of the family, find out who did this and set it right.

CAITLIN. Was he a large man?

MRS. SLATER. This was his belt. I wear it across my chest in his memory.

15

CAITLIN. *(Referring to the feet.)* They're so bloated.

MRS. SLATER. Just try, Gene. That's all I want.

GENE. How? It's been fourteen years! There's nothing to go on!

MRS. SLATER. Yes, there is. *(She pulls out another jar, this time with one foot floating in it.)*

CAITLIN. Jesus, it's another foot.

GENE. You have to stop this!

MRS. SLATER. Listen to me, Gene.

GENE. This is crazy! You have jars of feet!

MRS. SLATER. There's someone out there missing this foot and they know what happened to your father.

CAITLIN. *(Turning away suddenly.)* I'm sorry. I can't look at them anymore.

GENE. You're making my company sick.

CAITLIN. Especially the big ones. I can't —

MRS. SLATER. Stiffen up, girlie. Life is hard.

GENE. Mama, please …

MRS. SLATER. You don't know, Gene. I try to pull you up but you wanna stay down, way down tugging at my skirt like a little boy. Well, I can't make a man out of you. You gotta do it yourself.

CAITLIN. *(Opens the door.)* I gotta run.

GENE. Caitlin, I'm sorry.

CAITLIN. No, it's — I'll … I'll see you in class. *(Exits quickly.)*

GENE. You couldn't wait until we were alone?!

MRS. SLATER. Why? She seems all right. You think we can't trust her?

GENE. That's not my point!

MRS. SLATER. I didn't know what else to do.

GENE. Call the police.

MRS. SLATER. The police did all they could, Gene. It's up to you now. *(Gene leans in to look at his father's feet.)* Please, Gene. *(Lights fade.)*

Scene 6

Bar. Carl is at a table writing in his journal. There are a few empty shot glasses in front of him. We hear his voice.

VOICE OF CARL. It's just past one A.M. and I'm restless. I had to get out. I dreamt I was running barefoot through the wet streets of the city and I was being chased by a street cleaning truck. My legs were tired and the truck was getting closer and my bare feet were bloody. And I looked over my shoulder and in the driver's seat was that man, the plain man from the repair shop and he was eating yogurt and black bread and laughing at me and he bellowed, "Kill me, put me out of my misery and kill me! Before I kill you first!" And then I tripped over a homeless man and fell! I wanted to get up but the truck barreled into me, and I was spun around and dragged along the street, and so was the homeless man. The two of us, screaming, and spinning and brushing up the trash and dirty water with our bodies. That's when I woke up. On my way here I decided that something had to be done. I don't want to be chased by him anymore, chased by that worthless nobody. I don't want to be tormented. Tomorrow we were supposed to begin *Anna Karenina*. I'm afraid I may not be prepared to lecture. *(Caitlin appears in the distance. She looks at Carl and down at his journal. Carl does not see her.)*

Scene 7

Laundromat. Mrs. Slater is packing Gene's clothes into a large backpack. We hear the sound of dogs barking and chasing after someone. Lily runs into laundromat and closes the door quickly. She is out of breath, and carrying a sketch pad and a meat pie.

LILY. Those your dogs?

MRS. SLATER. Hell no.

LILY. They always out there?

MRS. SLATER. Since the strike.

LILY. *(Looking out the window.)* Something should be done about that. That's not safe, all those dogs out there.

MRS. SLATER. Hey, you're from that repair shop.

LILY. Uhh, that's right.

MRS. SLATER. My compass fixed?

LILY. I don't know. I just live there.

MRS. SLATER. Right. *(Beat.)* I think they wanted that pie.

LILY. What?

MRS. SLATER. The dogs. The must've smelled your pie.

LILY. Well they're not getting any. I've been craving this pie all day. I'm gonna stand right here and eat it. *(She does.)* You want some? It's mincemeat.

MRS. SLATER. You buy it at Schultzy's?

LILY. That's right.

MRS. SLATER. No thanks. Schultzy's food is no good. People get sick from it. *(Confidentially.)* I think there are things living in it. Unsanitary, microscopic organisms. *(Queasy, Lily tosses the pie outside. We hear the dogs devour it.)*

LILY. These dogs are terrible.

MRS. SLATER. They've taken over this side of the street. You read *The Post* yesterday?

LILY. No.

MRS. SLATER. A jogger was attacked by a German shepherd in Central Park. Tore off a piece of his thigh. Maybe they're turning against us.

LILY. The dogs?

MRS. SLATER. Happens all the time. When I was a girl we had a dog named Cracker, but we were so poor that we didn't have anything to feed him, so he lived out of the garbage, like these dogs. Even so, there's only so much an animal can take. One day he made a dash for my baby brother's crib, snatched him up in his teeth and ran with him. Cracker gorged himself in some back alley. *(Shows bit of blanket pinned to her sweater.)* This piece of baby blanket was all that was left.

LILY. Your brother was eaten by a dog?

MRS. SLATER. That's how it is in our family. Things like that just happen. There's something in the blood. Even the dog was run down by a garbage truck.

LILY. My father was run down by a garbage truck. Isn't that strange? Stuff like that happens in my family too. I mean, no one's ever been eaten but —

MRS. SLATER. You wanna sketch my feet?

LILY. I'm sorry?

MRS. SLATER. Your friend said you liked to draw feet.

LILY. Uh … all right.

MRS. SLATER *(Taking off shoes.)* Can I keep packing?

LILY. Sure. *(Settles in and starts sketching her feet.)*

MRS. SLATER. You know, I haven't done this sort of thing in years. Not since Jack and I had our portraits done at Coney Island.

LILY. Your toes are so hairy.

MRS. SLATER. I get that from my father. He was covered with hair from head to foot.

LILY. My father was bald.

MRS. SLATER. My father was an epileptic.

LILY. Really?

MRS. SLATER. A hairy epileptic. He worked as a clerk in a hat factory. And one morning he was going through a stack of invoices while cleaning his ears with a letter opener, and just at that moment he was struck with a fit. He flailed around a bit, threw his head onto the counter and rammed the opener up into his brain.

He left me this ring. *(Shows hand happily.)*

LILY. *(Trying to smile.)* Oh … It's … very beautiful. *(Pause.)* I have to tell you something. This is the strangest thing because … *(Looks around suddenly, runs to door and locks it, pulls down shades.)*

MRS. SLATER. What are you doing?

LILY. I feel like I can trust you. We have a lot in common, you and I. *(Secretively.)* Before my father died, he left me something as well.

MRS. SLATER. A ring?

LILY. No, it was a silver tie clip shaped like a beagle puppy. He wore it every day. And when I turned twelve, he gave it to me and said it would protect me. And then he went to pick up my birthday cake and on his way back he was run down by the garbage truck.

MRS. SLATER. Just like Cracker.

LILY. It was a tragic loss but at least I had that tie clip to remind me of him. And I never took it off, except once, in tenth grade when Salvatore Dento asked if he could wear it for fourteen seconds. I let him. That afternoon, two police officers had to tell me that the book binding factory where my mother worked had burned to the ground. They found her body under a smoldering set of encyclopedias. It occurred at precisely 1:23 P.M. — the exact time I handed the clip over to Salvatore Dento.

MRS. SLATER. That's an odd coincidence.

LILY. Yes, a little too odd. My sister Maureen and I were orphans. She had to take a job at Coney Island to support us, greasing the machinery under the tracks of the Cyclone. One exceptionally hot summer day, I was tanning myself on the beach, when a seagull plucked the tie clip from my bathing suit and tried to eat it. I managed to beat the bird silly and get it back, but in those few seconds, my sister's foot got caught in the tracks of the roller coaster and … I can't go on. I've said too much.

MRS. SLATER. No, please … continue.

LILY. I can't.

MRS. SLATER. All right.

LILY. Except this … That day, I realized that tie clip had mystical powers. And so long as I wore it everything was fine, but as soon as I took it off, horribly tragic things would occur. It took my entire family to die for me to realize that, but as soon as I did, that tie clip never left me, and life was almost bearable. And that's how it was, until someone stole it from me.

MRS. SLATER. Who?

LILY. I can't say. I don't want to involve you.

MRS. SLATER. Good, I'd rather you didn't.

LILY. It's been gone fourteen years, and in that time, all the people who have —

MRS. SLATER. I don't want to know. You'll jinx me.

LILY. I've come back to get it. I know it's here somewhere. I'm going to put an end to this suffering once and for all. *(Gene enters from upstairs.)*

MRS. SLATER. Oh, Gene, I want you to meet this woman who just ran in here.

LILY. Hello, I'm Lily.

MRS. SLATER. Like the flower, Gene. She's an artist. She's drawing my feet.

LILY. Your mother's an incredible woman.

GENE. Yes, I know.

LILY. We have a lot in common.

GENE. Do you? You should ask to see her collections.

LILY. Do you collect things?

MRS. SLATER. Thimbles. Nothing but thimbles. Gene, go to the basement and look around. I think there's a water leak somewhere. The floor's wet. *(Gene exits. Outside, we hear him lifting the metal grates that lead to the basement.)*

LILY. You won't tell anyone what I told you?

MRS. SLATER. Not a soul.

LILY. Good. *(Goes back to sketching.)* Your son seems nice.

MRS. SLATER. He is. A little naive, but nice.

LILY. *(Referring to backpack.)* Where's he going? Camping?

MRS. SLATER. No, he's going to find his father's killer. He hasn't agreed to go yet, but I think he'll come round soon. Make sure you get my ankles. Jack always said he liked my ankles. Jack's my husband. *(Beat.)* Hey, you like feet, you should see his. *(Goes to get the jar with Jack's feet.)* Jack had beautiful feet. They were fat, you understand, but beautiful. Since we're sharing and being so open and honest … *(Plunks jar in front of her.)* Nice, huh?

LILY. Oh … these … oh my goodness …

MRS. SLATER. He was cut up fourteen years ago in the

Poconos, but Gene'll find 'em. I had to wait until he was of age. I mean, we couldn't have some seven-year-old running around avenging his father.

LILY. *(Looking outside.)* Dogs are gone.

MRS. SLATER. They're afraid of Gene. He must give off some smell.

LILY. I should probably get going.

MRS. SLATER. What about my feet?

LILY. This is a good start. I really have a few things to do. *(Gene enters and nearly bumps into Lily.)*

GENE. Sorry.

LILY. No, I'm sorry. I … It was nice meeting you both. *(Exits quickly.)*

GENE. You scare her too?

MRS. SLATER. Leave me alone. You find the leak?

GENE. No, you should call someone about it.

MRS. SLATER. Who am I gonna call?

GENE. I'm gonna head over to Astor. *(Takes skateboard from behind door.)*

MRS. SLATER. I'm almost done packing, Gene. Don't be long.

GENE. I have class later. We'll talk tonight.

MRS. SLATER. No more talk, Gene. *(Gene exits with skateboard. Lights fade.)*

Scene 8

Subway car. Caitlin and Gene are standing.

GENE. You look tired.

CAITLIN. Yeah, well, I had nightmares about those damn feet all night. Your mother gives me the creeps.

GENE. I'm sorry about all that.

CAITLIN. You gonna go find who did it?

GENE. I don't know.

CAITLIN. I think you should. For your mother's sake. *(Caitlin takes Carl's journal out of her bag and hands it to Gene.)* Look what I did. It's Carl's journal. I stole it.
GENE. Apparently.
CAITLIN. You wouldn't believe what he's written in here. He's suffering. And he has terrible dreams, just like me.
GENE. He's gonna catch you.
CAITLIN. I hope he does catch me. I want him to. I love him now more than ever.
GENE. Oh yeah?
CAITLIN. And there are bits about his childhood, and about his marriage.
GENE. He was married?
CAITLIN. To a rock climber, but she was murdered. Eaten alive.
GENE. What?
CAITLIN. *(Flipping through book.)* Look. He has these articles pasted in here about a cult of cannibals. These ex-Wall Street types who turned on the world and started eating people.
GENE. I've never heard of that.
CAITLIN. Yeah, there are a couple cases in New Jersey, and one in Maryland.
GENE. And they ate his wife?
CAITLIN. That's what he says. At least he mentions it. Some of the pages are ripped out. It's a little confusing, but you should read it and try to figure it out.
GENE. I don't want to figure it out.
CAITLIN. And he talks about the guy from the repair shop. He's serious about killing him. He has plans, big plans.
GENE. He's unstable.
CAITLIN. I'm inexplicably pulled to him. That's how it is with women like me. Don't I remind you of Anna Karenina?
GENE. Not really.
CAITLIN. Say that I do. Tell me how much I remind you of her. Tell me I'm impetuous like her. And passionate and a little mysterious like her. And beautiful.
GENE. I thought she was kind of dumb. *(Caitlin slaps him.)* Ow.
CAITLIN. Don't ever speak of Anna like that again …
GENE. I'm sorry.

CAITLIN. What do you know anyway? Why do I even talk to you?

GENE. Because no one else would listen.

CAITLIN. Shut up. *(Noticing the doodles and notes on the cover of Gene's notebook.)* What is this?

GENE. It's a notebook.

CAITLIN. Why did you write all over it? *(Takes book and looks at it.)* What is this? German?

GENE. No, it's not German.

CAITLIN. What's Wcylmioh?

GENE. It's my secret thoughts.

CAITLIN. *(Reading.)* Ilcb. What is Ilcb?

GENE. It's not a word. It's ... from *Anna Karenina*. Each letter is a word in a sentence. You're suppose to guess.

CAITLIN. Is "I" idiot?

GENE. No.

CAITLIN. *(Trying to form words.)* Inkblots, igloos, incest ... incest looks crazy, boy.

GENE. No.

CAITLIN. Ismene ... likes cooked bacon. Interiors lack cruddy boars. Icky lips can break. I love cracking bones. I love catching bees.

GENE. You're getting warmer.

CAITLIN. I love cheese balls. I love cabbage, baby. I love cat ... *(Realizing.)* C.B. ... Those are my initials.

GENE. Caitlin ...

CAITLIN. Do you have a crush on me, Gene?

GENE. Look, I know you have this thing for Professor Raymonds and you don't even know me that well, and you slapped my face, which probably isn't a very good sign but —

CAITLIN. You don't want me, Gene. I have too much baggage. You want someone nice.

GENE. You are nice.

CAITLIN. No, I'm awful. There are things I should tell you, but I can't.

GENE. Why?

CAITLIN. Because I'm not supposed to. Because you haven't lived yet. You're a boy, Gene. I don't have anything to learn from you.

GENE. What are you talking about?

CAITLIN. I like people like me, people with baggage. You're so … carefree.

GENE. I'm not carefree. I have a lot on my mind.

CAITLIN. I'm sorry, Gene. *(Train jerks suddenly.)* God. We hit something. Someone must've thrown himself in front of the train. We'll probably be here awhile. *(Gene's looking off.)* You're not mad at me, are you, Gene? Gene? *(Lights fade.)*

Scene 9

Laundromat. Mrs. Slater is sewing Gene's rain slicker. We hear the familiar sound of the dogs barking and chasing after someone. Brad comes running in and slams door.

BRAD. Cripes! Those dogs are crazy. What's the matter with them?

MRS. SLATER. Ya fix my compass?

BRAD. They could've bit me.

MRS. SLATER. Your friend tell you I needed it?

BRAD. *(Hands her compass.)* Yeah, but she didn't mention the dogs.

MRS. SLATER. It's shiny. You polish it? *(Carl appears in the window, distraught. He's watching Brad.)*

BRAD. Yes ma'am. I take real pride in my work, as dull as it might be.

MRS. SLATER. *(Counting out quarters.)* Mind if I pay in quarters? *(We hear the dogs barking. Carl runs off. Brad turns around but doesn't see anything.)* How's your friend?

BRAD. She's not feeling too good. She ate some bad pie.

MRS. SLATER. I warned her, you know. You tell her that if she feels any better, she should stop by here. I gave myself a pedicure.

BRAD. *(Looking out window.)* Hey, the dogs ran off. I need to get over to Radio Shack before they close. See ya. *(He runs out. Mrs. Slater walks around testing the compass. Gene enters.)*

GENE. I'm going to the Poconos, Mama.

25

MRS. SLATER. You're what?

GENE. I need to be a man, you said it yourself. It's time I did something in life. I'm going to avenge my father's death.

MRS. SLATER. Oh, Gene … this is wonderful! I knew you'd come round!

GENE. I'm sorry I doubted you.

MRS. SLATER. You were very young. I couldn't tell you the truth back then.

GENE. But now I'm a man.

MRS. SLATER. Yes Gene, a man who's going to give me healthy grandchildren. (Goes to desk and pulls out a huge pair of shoes.) Here they are. Your father's walking shoes. He bought them specially for his trip. I want you to wear them.

GENE. Oh, I don't know …

MRS. SLATER. I stuffed balls of newspaper in the toes so they'd fit better. Here, try them on. If you lace them up tight, they'll fit close enough.

GENE. (Putting on shoes.) This is weird, Mama. He was wearing these when —

MRS. SLATER. He'd be so proud. (Shows him compass.) I had his compass fixed in case you got lost.

GENE. I need to know the roads he walked on.

MRS. SLATER. (Bustles around and pulls maps and brochures out of desk drawer.) I've saved all his maps. His whole route was charted out. They gave me everything he left with. Everything except that scarf. If you can find the scarf, Gene, it would mean so much to me. It belonged to my mother. I used to wear it in her memory. But it's gone now. And here's the brochure he gave me for The Honey Pine Inn. We were supposed to take the bus down and meet him there to celebrate some of his progress.

GENE. And before he left he bought me that raft.

MRS. SLATER. The raft for the lake. You held it on your lap the whole way down. And the inn was so beautiful. And I was in that little room, waiting for those big old shoes to walk in. I thought how I would unlace them and massage his tired feet and tell him what a wonderful and brave man he was, and how thin he was looking. I sat on the end of that bed and I could hear you out back where one of the innkeepers' children was teaching you how to skateboard, do you remember?

GENE. A little bit.

MRS. SLATER. That was lucky, wasn't it? At least something good came out of all that. You do tricks for people now and they throw money at you. Good pocket money. And you learned it in the mountains.

GENE. Not anymore, Mama. Tonight's the last time.

MRS. SLATER. You're a man now.

GENE. And only kids ride skateboards.

MRS. SLATER. *(Drags out the backpack.)* I packed all your clothes. I hope it's not too heavy.

GENE. *(Indicating shoes.)* How do they look?

MRS. SLATER. Wonderful. Walk around in them. Oh, you look so grown up. My big boy in his big daddy's shoes. You're gonna find whoever did it, Gene. There's no room in the world for a person who kills an innocent man. No room at all. *(Lights fade on Gene walking in shoes.)*

Scene 10

Bar. Carl is sitting at a table, smoking. He is writing madly on a stack of napkins.

VOICE OF CARL. He stole my journal. He snuck in here when I wasn't looking and swiped it from me. Now he knows. Goddam that boring, worthless swill. I can't sleep anymore. I can't lecture.

CAITLIN. Professor Raymonds? Your lecture was wonderful. *Anna Karenina* is my favorite novel.

CARL. Who are you? What do you want?

CAITLIN. I'm Caitlin Boyd. I'm in your Russian Lit class.

CARL. I can't talk to you.

CAITLIN. Your lectures arouse me.

CARL. I need some private time right now.

CAITLIN. But I wanted to tell you I've been in love with you since October. *(Pause, and then suddenly:)* I'm sorry. I swore I wouldn't say it.

CARL. What's your name?

CAITLIN. Caitlin.

CARL. Caitlin, I don't have the time. You think you're the first student to have a crush on me? Everyone has a crush on me. Go to the poetry professors. They like that sort of thing.

CAITLIN. You want me to go away, but I can't. Something is pulling me towards you. You scare me, and I love that you do. I love that you scare me. I love you.

CARL. Please, I need to be alone. I am a sick man. I am an angry man. I am an unattractive man. I think there might be something wrong with my liver.

CAITLIN. *(Drops journal in front of him.)* This is yours. Your writing is very sketchy. You leave parts out. Pages are missing.

CARL. Where did you get this?

CAITLIN. I stole it.

CARL. But I thought —

CAITLIN. You thought it was the repairman. *(Beat.)* It's wonderful. I made xeroxes of the most interesting pages. I tacked them around my bed so I could go to sleep with your words swirling around me. I want to help you.

CARL. You shouldn't steal things from people.

CAITLIN. You shouldn't plan a murder.

CARL. I'm not planning a murder.

CAITLIN. You can't get it out of your head. Let me help you kill him. I want to. I want to kill him. I want to lead a horrible and passionate life. I want to be like you.

CARL. Go home. Read a book.

CAITLIN. I'll go to the police, professor.

CARL. You're a very funny young woman.

CAITLIN. Let me help you. I'll tell everyone if you don't. I'll do whatever you want. Let me help. Let me. Let me, please. *(She leans forward and kisses him full on the mouth. He is surprised at first and then leans into the kiss. Lights fade.)*

Scene 11

Appliance repair shop. Lily is on the phone. The Yellow Pages are open in front of her. She looks tired and ill.

LILY. *(On telephone.)* He'd be wearing a tie clip shaped like a puppy ... You don't? ... All right, keep your eyes open and maybe I'll call back. *(Hangs up and dials next phone number in the* Yellow Pages.*)* Leonard's Pub? I'm looking for a man who may spend some time there. He might be wearing a puppy tie clip and his name — *(Brad enters with bag from Radio Shack and Lily hangs up suddenly.)*

BRAD. Who were you talking to?

LILY. Nobody. How was Radio Shack?

BRAD. *(Puts bag down.)* Great. I love that place. You look awful. Why don't you go lie down and I'll make you some soup or something?

LILY. That's really sweet, Brad, but maybe a little later.

BRAD. All right. I wanted to get over to Astor anyway. I just passed by and that skateboarder says he's giving a farewell performance. I wanted to maybe catch the end of it. *(Pause.)* I started a story. It's about the laughing devil head that lives in my wallpaper. It's a children's story.

LILY. That sounds different.

BRAD. There's a little girl who lives in the woods and a devil floats off the wall and starts talking to her. But he's a friendly devil and made of wallpaper.

LILY. *(Nose in* Yellow Pages.*)* I'm sorry, Brad, but I'm trying to concentrate here.

BRAD. What are you doing?

LILY. Nothing. I have to do a few things so I can leave.

BRAD. Leave? Are you leaving already?

LILY. Well not right away, but soon.

BRAD. I wish I could just take off. Like you. Or like the skateboarder. He says he's going to the Poconos.

LILY. What?

BRAD. Yeah, isn't that weird? He's going to the Poconos. He didn't say why, but it's still a little strange.

LILY. Why? People go to the Poconos all the time.

BRAD. But don't you think it's a coincidence? I mean, you just show up on my doorstep, looking for a place to stay and I can't help but think of the Poconos. I only know you from the Poconos. We met in the Poconos, drove away from the Poconos. So I'm thinking about the Poconos, the Poconos, and all that blood in the Poconos. I mean, the whole encounter really stuck with me.

LILY. Brad, please.

BRAD. And then this young man announces that he's going to the Poconos. Again, the Poconos. What is it with that place?

LILY. I don't know! *(Phone rings. Brad answers it.)*

BRAD. Brad's Fix-it Shop ... Hello? ... Hello? ... They hung up. *(He's suddenly struck with an itch above his right ankle and scratches at it madly.)* Oh God, I got one of those itches again. I hate that. *(He pulls up pant leg and reveals that his right foot is prosthetic. He scratches around where prosthetic foot is attached.)* You'd think they'd come out with a prosthetic foot that didn't itch. What were we talking about?

LILY. I don't remember.

BRAD. Yes, you do. We were talking about how we met in the Poconos.

LILY. Really, I'm not feeling well.

BRAD. You should go lie down. I'll lock up and go watch the skateboarder.

LILY. I've thrown up six times today.

BRAD. But can I ask you one thing before you go in?

LILY. What, Brad? *(Brad goes to workbench and drags out a huge ceramic foot with newspaper articles pasted all over it.)*

BRAD. What is this?

LILY. Where did you get that?

BRAD. In your closet. I was looking for some fuses.

LILY. There are no fuses in my closet.

BRAD. I know that now.

LILY. It's one of my sculptures.

BRAD. But it has all these newspaper articles pasted all over it.

LILY. It's supposed to.

BRAD. *(Reading article titles.)* "Mutilated Fat Man Found in The Poconos," "A Third Unknown Foot Discovered Under Rocks," "Fatty's Stroll Footloose But Not Fancy Free!"

LILY. It's a motif, Brad!

BRAD. But this happened fourteen years ago, on the same day that I picked you up hitchhiking in the Poconos.

LILY. Stay out of my things, please. I don't question you, so please treat me with the same respect.

BRAD. I'm just curious.

LILY. And I'm not feeling well. I'll be gone in a few days, I wish you'd just give me some room.

BRAD. I'm sorry. *(Lily goes to ceramic foot to see if any damage was done. She picks it up.)*

LILY. I don't mean to be snippy. It's my stomach. I'll talk to you when I'm feeling a little better. *(Walks into her room with ceramic foot. Brad looks at doorway. After a couple beats, he reaches into his jacket pocket and pulls out an old, flowered, silk scarf that is stained with blood. Brad opens it up and examines it closely as the lights fade. Blackout.)*

Scene 12

Carl's van. Carl is sitting in the driver's seat with a gun. Caitlin is looking out the passenger's side window with a pair of binoculars. She picks up a camera and takes several shots.

CARL. You see him?

CAITLIN. Yeah.

CARL. Plain, isn't he?

CAITLIN. This is the guy who's gonna kill you?

CARL. He's gonna kill me all right. My dreams are like premonitions.

CAITLIN. Mine too.

CARL. Oh God, he makes my skin crawl! Look at him!

CAITLIN. Oh, you're all fired up. Can we go back to your room … lover?

CARL. What?

CAITLIN. Back to that little hovel you live in with all those books? All those papers scattered across your bed, that bottle of vodka on the nightstand? Can we share another cigarette, professor?

CARL. No.

CAITLIN. All right. *(Looks through binoculars.)* Oh God, he makes my skin crawl! Look at him! *(Trying to sound mysterious.)* That's his pad. He steps out at exactly 8:50 A.M. every morning, heads to the corner for a raspberry tart and a cup o' jo, gets back, lines up his tools like they were precious gems, and opens shop at nine on the nose. That's his daily M.O.

CARL. What are you talking about?

CAITLIN. This is very exciting. We're really gonna do it. We're gonna let him have it. Pop him. Do him real quiet like, right?

CARL. All right, outta the van. This was a big mistake.

CAITLIN. No, I'll be good. You just let me know when. I'm just so excited. We're gonna snuff him out like Raskolnikov did!

CARL. Here, switch places. Can you drive?

CAITLIN. *(Awkwardly climbing over him.)* Uh … yeah, I can drive. Careful of the gun. You don't wanna shoot me.

CARL. Oh yeah?

CAITLIN. You're very witty, Carl. I love your wit.

CARL. *(Looking through binoculars.)* This is good. I have a clear shot of him.

CAITLIN. Do I remind you of Anna Karenina?

CARL. She's fictional.

CAITLIN. Right, but do I remind you of her?

CARL. No. Hold on. He's leaving the shop. Stay close.

CAITLIN. I know that I do. You're just saying that I don't. *(Pulls out van.)* Ooo, we're trailing him. Trailing the fix-it man. On the trail of the fix-it man.

CARL. Shut up.

CAITLIN. He's walking so fast. Must be late for something.

CARL. Go around the block. We'll cut him off.

CAITLIN. Did your wife drive?

CARL. Who said I had a wife?

CAITLIN. I read it, remember? She was a rock climber, right?

CARL. That's none of your business.

CAITLIN. But she turned against you, accused you of being obsessive and crazy.

CARL. I was.

CAITLIN. Your writing is vague.

CARL. It's my journal. I can write what I want.

CAITLIN. But from what I understand, her dream in life was to climb Gorey Cliff, the sheerest rock face in the whole Pennsylvania Poconos!

CARL. We're losing him!

CAITLIN. And that's where she went when she left you, but she never climbed that rock face because she was murdered!

CARL. Please!

CAITLIN. Was she really eaten by someone or did you kill her?!

CARL. What?!

CAITLIN. Did you kill your rock-climbing wife?!

CARL. No! She went there and she was eaten!

CAITLIN. I love you, Carl! Even if you didn't murder your wife, even if you won't let me run this man down, I still love you!

CARL. There he is!

CAITLIN. Where?!

CARL. There, by the parking lot!

CAITLIN. He's heading for that crowd of people!

CARL. Hurry up! I want to see what he's doing!

CAITLIN. What are those trash baskets?

CARL. Keep going!

CAITLIN. There's a red light!

CARL. Go through it!

CAITLIN. I can't!

CARL. Go through it! *(Caitlin screams. The van hits something.)* Where'd he go?

CAITLIN. We hit a skateboarder!

CARL. Just keep going!

CAITLIN. It's Gene! We gotta go back!

CARL. I said to keep going! Go! Go! *(Blackout.)*

End of Act One

ACT TWO

Scene 1

Appliance repair shop. Lily, in pain and a bit dazed, is reading Dostoyevsky's Nightmares. *She's eating a protein bar. Brad, exhausted, enters with a big bandage around his head.*

LILY. Well look at you, up and about. How's your head?

BRAD. It has a dent in it.

LILY. You look awful.

BRAD. So do you.

LILY. My stomach is worse.

BRAD. I haven't slept in five days. Too much on my mind. It keeps me awake at night. That poor skateboarder had his whole life ahead of him. He performs there every day. Crosses the same streets. Jumps over the same baskets. And then one day someone goes through a red light and runs him down.

LILY. It's too bad about the skateboard.

BRAD. *(Exiting into back.)* I need to get some ice.

LILY. Flying up and hitting you in the head.

BRAD. *(Off.)* Yeah, my noggin's all outta sorts now. I can't put two and two together.

LILY. You should see someone about that.

BRAD. But I did remember something. *(Enters with a bag of ice.)* When the van drove by, there was a guy leaning out the passenger side window with a gun. I don't know what that skateboarder did to him, but I think he wanted to kill him. He had this crazy look in his eye.

LILY. You should give a description to the police.

BRAD. Yeah ... because ... I know that guy. I know him somehow. He ... If my head was right I'd remember. He ... *(Has sudden*

34

pain in his head.) He used to …

LILY. You all right?

BRAD. I get these waves of pain. That's what's keeping me awake. I can't even write. My children's story is going nowhere.

LILY. You should go see an acupuncturist.

BRAD. I was brushing my hair in the mirror this morning and I saw the devil waving at me from inside the corner of my eyeball. The devil was banging his tiny fists on the inside of my eye and laughing at me. Whaddaya make of that?

LILY. You got whacked hard. *(There's a series of camera flashes at the window as Caitlin snaps a few Polaroids and runs off.)* Who was that?

BRAD. Must be tourists. *(Notices her book.)* What's that you're reading?

LILY. Nothing.

BRAD. *Dostoyevsky's Nightmares?* How weird. I … I just … I'll be right back. *(Exits into back room suddenly.)*

LILY. Where are you going?

BRAD. *(Off.)* I used to read Dostoyevsky back in college. All the Russian writers. Then I gave it all up. All of it. Now I just take things apart. *(Enters with stack of dusty old books.)* I've kept these in my closet. Wanna look?

LILY. No, keep them away from me! I don't wanna — *(Brad spots the picture of Carl on the back of Lily's book.)*

BRAD. Carl Raymonds!

LILY. What?!

BRAD. He's gotten so old. This was my Russian Literature professor. Carl Raymonds!

LILY. Carl?!

BRAD. Yes! The other day, he was peeking through my window and there was something familiar about him, but I couldn't remember.

LILY. Carl Raymonds?!

BRAD. Plus I got whacked by the skateboard and my head's all messed up and I'm seeing this wallpaper devil and everything.

LILY. Professor Carl Raymonds?!

BRAD. And he was the one in the van trying to kill that boy!

LILY. Brad, Professor Carl Raymonds was obsessed with me. He said he loved me. He followed me through the streets. That's why

35

I moved to Florida. I went to art school in St. Petersburg, but my pottery instructor died in a kiln explosion, six graduate students were all crushed under a falling industrial sculpture and my silk screen teacher swallowed a gallon of turpentine. I don't know how it happened, but I know why, damnit. Three weeks ago, I was in a bookstore near the beach and I came across this book! See the picture? See what he's wearing?

BRAD. A suit?

LILY. A tie clip! A tie clip shaped like a little beagle!

BRAD. It's cute.

LILY. Cute?! This goddam cute clip has destroyed my life and the lives of anyone I've ever come in contact with! You think it's so cute that you're seeing wallpaper devils in the bathroom mirror?!

BRAD. He's a nice devil.

LILY. I've called every bar in the city trying to find him, because I remember he liked to drink. But so far nothing. And even if I *do* find him, I have to get the clip without him knowing it. Because if he sees me — *(Sudden pain in stomach.)* And now my stomach isn't right. The tie clip is trying to kill me, the way it ran down my father, and burned my mother and drowned my sister! Something's growing in my stomach!

BRAD. I have a devil in my eyeball.

LILY. And Carl's found me! He's not trying to kill that boy. He's trying to kill me. *(Blackout.)*

Scene 2

Laundromat. Mrs. Slater and Gene are sitting in silence. Gene's in a wheelchair, paralyzed from the waist down, and slightly dazed. Mrs. Slater is wearing Gene's skateboard around her neck in memoriam to his legs. She's holding a dinner plate with food and utensils on her lap. The jar with Mr. Slater's feet in it sits on the desk.

MRS. SLATER. It's in the blood. Tragedy courses through our veins. It's in the family, Gene. It runs under our skin like an earthworm chewing its way to the surface. It seizes us, shakes us up. It cripples us and rots us from the inside out, and nothing's to be done. There's a cancer in the family and look what it leaves behind. Mementos. Life's junk. It took your legs. And your father's beautiful feet. Someone's responsible and we're going to find them. *(Goes to him with plate of food.)* But you can't starve yourself, Gene. It isn't right. Take a bite for me. Please. *(Makes several tries to feed him, but he turns his head away each time.)* You're being very stubborn. Now please, take a bite.

GENE. *(Grabs plate, throws it across the room.)* I don't want this fucking swill! Don't bring it to me!

MRS. SLATER. That was very bad. You're being a very bad boy.

GENE. *(Sees jar of feet.)* What are you doing with my father's feet?

MRS. SLATER. I was looking at them.

GENE. Put them away.

MRS. SLATER. You're angry with me, aren't you?

GENE. I'm just sick of looking at things like that.

MRS. SLATER. All right, I'll put them in the basement.

GENE. *(Wheeling himself towards the jar.)* I'll do it myself. *(Gene picks up jar and exits with it while his mother is talking.)*

MRS. SLATER. You can't go down there, Gene. The water's up to my knees. You'll short circuit your chair. I built you a ramp. It goes down from the sidewalk. I have blisters from the hammering.

37

And one of the dogs bit me. But I think it's a nice ramp. I hope you like it. But you shouldn't go down there, Gene. *(There is a sudden crash of the jar breaking on the street outside, then the sound of the dogs barking and tearing away at the feet. After a couple beats, Gene enters, numbed.)*

GENE. I dropped my father's feet. They broke on the sidewalk. The dogs smelled meat. Formaldehyde and meat. *(Mrs. Slater rummages through her pants and pulls out a revolver.)*

MRS. SLATER. This is the gun that my mother used to shoot herself. I keep it in my pants in her memory. *(She turns, runs outside and begins shooting at the ravenous dogs. After several shots, she returns calmly.)* They ran, the cowards. Good legs on those dogs. They ate your father's feet. *(Begins to cry suddenly.)*

GENE. *(Gently.)* Mama, don't cry, please … it makes me weak … I'm sorry I dropped them … Please, Mama … *(His tone slowly changes to anger.)* Mama … stop it … Don't cry … I said … Would you fucking listen to me? … Who are you to cry? … What have you got to cry about? You have your legs. What do I have? I have nothing! I've lost everything. I'm a half person! I lost my legs, Mama. I lost my dick, Mama. I have nothing, no feeling. *(He grabs steak knife.)* It's nothing. It's dead meat! *(Gene starts stabbing himself in the legs.)* Look, Mama! This is what I'm worth! I can't feel it! I've lost it! *(His mother screams and tries to wrestle the knife from his hands. There is a standoff as she holds his arm, while he tries to plunge it into his leg again.)*

MRS. SLATER. Stop it! You're just feeling sorry for yourself.

GENE. Let go!

MRS. SLATER. That's my good carving knife, Gene. *(She bites his hand and manages to get knife away from him. He grabs at knife and falls out of the chair.)* Goddamit. *(Gene's legs are bleeding. He's dragging himself around the laundromat as he heads to his wheelchair.)*

GENE. I don't have anything, Mama. I haven't lived and I don't have anything. Look at me. I'm nothing. *(She moves in close to him.)*

MRS. SLATER. Don't say that. You're something. You're *something.* And you have me. And hope. You have to go on. I did. Please, Gene. *(Lights fade.)*

38

Scene 3

Lecture hall. Carl's lecture is over. He is packing up his papers when Caitlin approaches him.

CAITLIN. Carl ...

CARL. Go away.

CAITLIN. Gene's paralyzed. He's in a wheelchair.

CARL. Why did you have to sign up for my class?

CAITLIN. It was fate pushing us together.

CARL. I never want to see you again. You shouldn't have gotten involved. I never would've gone through with it otherwise.

CAITLIN. I want to finish it. We had a plan.

CARL. Forget it. Sometimes I get stupid ideas. I need to get some help. Now leave me alone.

CAITLIN. I'll go to the police!

CARL. Go ahead! Find one! They're all hidden away in some giant warehouse where they've stockpiled donuts and fried egg sandwiches!

CAITLIN. What?

CARL. There aren't any cops anymore. Or trash collectors. The garbage is piling up! They've saved themselves. I had a dream. They're hibernating until this whole thing is over.

CAITLIN. What thing?

CARL. The sinking! The city is sinking! It's slipping under water! Don't you watch the news? They've closed the FDR Drive!

CAITLIN. For repairs.

CARL. Not for repairs. That's what they're telling you. That's what they want you to think, but Manhattan is slipping under water. Maybe you don't know it, but the police do and the trash collectors. All the city workers got the word. They escaped and they're not telling us unimportant people anything. But *I* know and the cockroaches and the dogs. They're all going crazy. They sense it. Like cows that know a cyclone is coming. They know!

CAITLIN. You're just trying to brush me off, you naughty thing. *(Pulling photos out of pocket.)* I took some photos.

CARL. Are you not listening to me?

CAITLIN. There's a woman living with him. Look. *(Something in the photo stops Carl dead in his tracks. He grabs photo and looks at it.)*

CARL. Oh my God.

CAITLIN. It must be his girlfriend. Maybe he's not as dull as we thought.

CARL. She's dyed her hair but ... she's —

CAITLIN. Carl?

CARL. She's supposed to be ... She's ... she's dead.

CAITLIN. Who is?

CARL. Lily.

CAITLIN. You know her?

CARL. It's Lily.

CAITLIN. The rock climber?

CARL. This is ... this is ... this is my wife. *(Blackout.)*

Scene 4

Appliance repair shop. Brad is wearing the bandage on his head and an eyepatch over his left eye. He is trying to ride his skateboard. Lily comes out of her bedroom quickly with her sketchpad under her arm. She is sealing an envelope as she enters.

LILY. If Carl comes by here, get the tie clip. Buy it from him. I'll pay you back. Any price. Just don't tell him where I am.

BRAD. Where are you going?

LILY. I have something to drop off. Why are you wearing that eyepatch?

BRAD. I was trying to write a couple hours ago, and the devil chewed his way through my optic nerve, crawled out of my nose and perched himself on top of my dresser. He sang a song about a prostitute named Dolly. He has a beautiful voice. I should add that to my story.

LILY. Try to rest, Brad.

BRAD. I don't think it can be a children's story anymore though. You see, he's not really the friendly wallpaper devil that I thought he was. Sure, he's made out of wallpaper, but he's not happy about it. In fact, he's a very angry devil. And he's been pushing me around, trying to get me to do things. And he's gotten much bigger.

LILY. All right, I'll be back in a bit. I'm not sure how much longer I have though. Whatever's inside me, is killing me. If I don't get that tie clip, I'm dead. I'll see you in a while. *(Exits.)*

BRAD. *(Turns as if he sees someone.)* I see you were eavesdropping. Well, I don't care. You're just a piece of wallpaper, so fuck off!

CAITLIN. *(Enters.)* Good morning.

BRAD. *(Turns around surprised.)* Oh, I … thought you were someone else. Can I … help you?

CAITLIN. Maybe. I'm looking for someone. Is there a rock climber living here with you? Name's Lily?

BRAD. Yeah, there's a Lily living here but she's an artist.

CAITLIN. So she's not a rock climber?

BRAD. She's an artist!

CAITLIN. Is she here?

BRAD. No, you just missed her.

CAITLIN. Damn. *(Beat.)* What happened to your head?

BRAD. I was hit by a skateboard.

CAITLIN. What's with your eye?

BRAD. A devil chewed his way through the back of it.

CAITLIN. And your foot?

BRAD. What?

CAITLIN. I was looking through that window this morning and I saw you take off your foot and scratch the stump.

BRAD. It gets itchy.

CAITLIN. Where's your missing foot?

BRAD. That's none of your business!

CAITLIN. Is it in a jar?!

BRAD. A jar?!

CAITLIN. Yes, a jar!

BRAD. No, it's gone! I was just a baby! My father was giving me a bath in the kitchen sink and he hit the switch to the garbage disposal by accident! It chewed off my foot!

CAITLIN. I see. When do you expect your friend back?

BRAD. She really doesn't tell me much.

CAITLIN. A bit of advice. Stay away from her. She'll steal your heart and leave you flappin' in the wind. And even after she's gone, maybe even dead and buried, she'll still be inside you, waiting to pop again and take you over. And when that happens, everything else will become insignificant and worthless, and ... pushed aside. That's what she'll do to a man. Believe me, I've seen it happen. And something's gotta be done about that, and I'm the one who's gonna do it.

BRAD. Are you a cop?

CAITLIN. Well ... Yes. Yes, I am. Now let me explain something to you. A young man was struck by a van and he's in a wheelchair.

BRAD. Oh.

CAITLIN. Exactly my reaction. He's a sweet kid and I'm not gonna rest until this case is cracked. The boy's dad was eighty-sixed in an equally violent way fourteen years ago in the Poconos.

BRAD. The Poconos?

CAITLIN. The Poconos.

BRAD. The Poconos!

CAITLIN. Yes, and someone involved is missing a foot.

BRAD. But they're missing a left foot, and I'm missing a right foot.

CAITLIN. How do you know that?

BRAD. I'm ... not at liberty to say.

CAITLIN. Uh-huh. What's your name? *(Picks up electric knife.)*

BRAD. Brad.

CAITLIN. *(Clicks on knife.)* You're very dull, Brad. What if someone killed you right now?

BRAD. Officer, please. I don't understand these questions.

CAITLIN. Would anyone notice?

BRAD. My father would. He's in a home down in St. Pete. He expects my call every Sunday. He's blind, and I'm the only family he has.

CAITLIN. I bet it's a dull family.

BRAD. Well, we're happy ... mostly.

CAITLIN. A happy dull family.

BRAD. *(Clutches head, turns his back on her.)* I've been having these headaches …

CAITLIN. *(Raising knife above her.)* All happy families are alike. *(About to sink knife into the back of his neck.)*

BRAD. But each unhappy family is unhappy in its own way.

CAITLIN. *(Stops suddenly.)* What?

BRAD. *Anna Karenina*! *(Facing Caitlin.)* Do you know Tolstoy?

CAITLIN. Yes!

BRAD. The opening line to *Anna Karenina*. "All happy families are alike … "

CAITLIN and BRAD. "But each unhappy family is unhappy in its own way"!

CAITLIN. Yes!

BRAD. You remind me of her. Your whole … the way you … You're very much like her.

CAITLIN. *(Kisses Brad suddenly.)* You're not dull. You're very exciting.

BRAD. That's what the devil's been saying to me.

CAITLIN. He's right, Brad!

BRAD. Oh, I used to love *Anna Karenina*, but I … I can't read those books anymore.

CAITLIN. You *should*. You *should* read them.

BRAD. I can't. I fell in love with my Russian Lit professor, but he never noticed me. I would go up to him after class, but he never knew who I was. Sometimes, I even followed him, but I was too plain for him to notice. It broke my heart. Even now he doesn't remember me, but *I* remember *him*. It took me awhile, but I remember. And so does Lily. He stole her tie clip. Isn't it a small world? *(Turns to invisible devil.)* What do you want? … Leave me alone, I'm talking to a cop! *(Turns back to Caitlin.)* He wants me to go find Carl. He's the one you want. I saw him run that boy down. I used to love Carl, but not anymore. Not after all that he's done.

CAITLIN. *(Backing to exit.)* I'm sorry I kissed you. Your insight was overwhelming. But now I realize that we're too similar. You make me feel sad and pathetic.

BRAD. Officer?

CAITLIN. I'm sorry, but I have to go do something very important that I can not tell you about. *(Exits shop quickly.)*

BRAD. Don't you wanna question Satan? *(To devil.)* Of course she believes us. She's a cop! We'll prove it! We'll gather evidence and bring it to her! *(Carl enters suddenly and slams the door.)* Officer! Officer come back!

CARL. Where is she?

BRAD. She who? I don't know any "shes."

CARL. My wife. She's living here with you. Are you screwing Lily?

BRAD. I'm not screwing anybody!

CARL. You think it'll last? Well, it won't, believe me!

BRAD. She didn't say you were married. She just —

CARL. If I didn't have a motive, I'd kill you.

BRAD. What?

CARL. Look at you, living your sickening and paltry little life. You don't know what life is. You know where I was found as a baby? In an alley! Wrestled from the teeth of a starving dog! A couple on their way back from the opera scraped me up and raised me as if I was their own. But you know who I belong to? Nobody!

BRAD. That's sad.

CARL. And I'm an epileptic! Are you?!

BRAD. No.

CARL. I didn't think so!

BRAD. Your wife —

CARL. You just tell her I want to talk about things.

BRAD. *(Looking out window.)* Is that your van over there?

CARL. Sure it's my van. You recognize it?

BRAD. You ran down that innocent boy!

CARL. What are you gonna do about it?

BRAD. Nothing. I don't suppose I could buy that tie clip?

CARL. You tell her I'll be at Nelson's Bar. It's three blocks over. *(Exits.)*

BRAD. He doesn't remember me! I gave him the biggest crush of my life and that's what I get in return! Let's call the cops. *(Goes to phone and dials 911.)* It's busy! The van? We can't search the van. *(The devil drags him to the door.)* Stop pulling on me! All right, I'll go! Let go of me! *(Brad is dragged out the door. Lights fade.)*

Scene 5

Laundromat. Mrs. Slater is here. Lily rushes in with sketch pad. Maybe a bit of blood from her stomach has seeped through her shirt. She is out of breath.

MRS. SLATER. I don't want to be sketched. Go away.

LILY. I just came to say goodbye.

MRS. SLATER. Where are you going?

LILY. Just ... away. Why are you wearing that skateboard?

MRS. SLATER. Gene was hit by a van, lost the use of his legs and stabbed himself several times. He's starving himself to be spiteful, but he's all right.

LILY. Do you remember that mincemeat I ate?

MRS. SLATER. I told you it was bad.

LILY. There's something growing inside me. It's eating me up.

MRS. SLATER. There's two feet of water in my basement. Who do I call about that?

LILY. I have consumption! I'm being consumed!

MRS. SLATER. Maybe you should sit down.

LILY. I can't. I gotta go. I just wanted to give you — *(Lily's about to give her the sketchpad when Caitlin enters wearing a dramatic cape with a fur lined collar.)*

CAITLIN. I'm here to see Gene.

MRS. SLATER. Oh, hello Juanita.

CAITLIN. Is Gene at home?

MRS. SLATER. This is my friend Lily. She sketches feet.

CAITLIN. Oh ... hello.

LILY. Hi.

CAITLIN. May I please speak to Gene?

MRS. SLATER. I'll go get him.

LILY. But I wanted to give you something.

MRS. SLATER. I'll be back in a minute. *(Exits. There is an uncomfortable pause as the two women look each other over.)*

45

LILY. Why are you looking at me like that?

CAITLIN. May I try something?

LILY. Such as? *(Caitlin calmly walks over to Lily, stares into her eyes, and suddenly stomps on her left foot. Lily has no reaction. Caitlin quickly stomps on it several times and then slowly walks away. Lily has felt nothing.)*

CAITLIN. Just as I suspected! You have a fake foot!

LILY. Yes, and you probably shouldn't stomp on it. Prosthetics are expensive.

CAITLIN. How did you lose your foot?

LILY. What do you mean?

CAITLIN. It seems everyone I know is missing feet! How did you lose yours?

LILY. I was hiking and there was a rock slide, and my foot got stuck. I called for help but no one heard me. I was high up.

CAITLIN. High up where? Where were you climbing?

LILY. None of your business.

CAITLIN. Was it the Poconos? On your way to Gorey Cliff?

LILY. Yes, but how — ?

CAITLIN. And no one heard you because of the altitude, and it was wooded and deserted.

LILY. That's right.

CAITLIN. And you couldn't get your foot free.

LILY. Yes! I screamed for three days. And I was dehydrated and starving. My pack was out of reach. The only things around me were an empty canteen and an ax.

CAITLIN. Ah, the ax!

LILY. Three days without food or water ... I ... took the ax and chopped my foot off. Somewhere in that mess I lost my tie clip. I left my foot under the rocks and dragged myself downhill.

CAITLIN. Where you met a fat man! *(Lily stares at Caitlin, grabs her by the throat and pushes her up against a dryer.)*

LILY. Who *are* you? *(Mrs. Slater wheels in Gene. His legs are bandaged and bloody.)*

MRS. SLATER. Look who's here everybody. It's Mr. Sunshine.

LILY. I have to go. Please, take these. *(Hands her sketchpad and letter.)* These are the sketches I did of your feet. I think they're pretty good. And the letter, don't open it until after I've gone, wait a couple days. *(To Gene.)* I'm sorry about what happened. Goodbye. *(Exits.)*

MRS. SLATER. What an odd bird. *(Puts letter in her pocket.)*

CAITLIN. Could we have a moment alone?

MRS. SLATER. Oh, a little hanky panky planned? I'll be upstairs if you need me? Just give a holler. *(Exits upstairs.)*

CAITLIN. It's good to see you, Gene. You're looking well.

GENE. Fuck off.

CAITLIN. It's too bad about all this. You're the last person to deserve it. *(Lights up a cigarette.)* You don't think I'm worthless, do you? I'm an exciting, desirable woman, aren't I? Tell me I am.

GENE. Since when do you smoke?

CAITLIN. *(Fiddling with book of matches.)* It's a habit I've picked up. It relaxes me.

GENE. *(Noticing matches.)* What's that?

CAITLIN. What?

GENE. Those matches.

CAITLIN. These matches?

GENE. I thought I saw something. Let me look at them.

CAITLIN. Here. *(Tosses him matches.)* I think I'm going away, Gene. Far away from here. Away with my lover.

GENE. *(Looks at matches.)* Where did you get these?

CAITLIN. At home. We have boxes of them.

GENE. These matches are from The Honey Pine Inn. In the Poconos.

CAITLIN. My parents used to own the place.

GENE. We stayed at The Honey Pine Inn when my father was killed. We were going to meet him there. I learned how to skateboard.

CAITLIN. Yes, I know. I taught you.

GENE. You taught me?

CAITLIN. I told you that you looked familiar, Gene. And then when your mother pulled out those feet … it all came back to me.

GENE. What are you talking about?

CAITLIN. I'm the innkeeper's daughter. We practiced skateboarding in the driveway, remember?

GENE. I don't believe this. Why didn't you tell me before?

CAITLIN. There's a lot you don't know about me. The Poconos

is only the tip of it!

GENE. Caitlin ...

CAITLIN. We left the mountains to get away from things. I was very young and I had an experience that left me traumatized. You see, I witnessed a murder.

GENE. What murder?

CAITLIN. Your father's murder.

GENE. My father? How do you know?

CAITLIN. I just know.

GENE. You should've told me! What did you see?

CAITLIN. It's in my nightmares. It's messed me up inside. I was only six.

GENE. Who did it?

CAITLIN. I was in my little bed and I heard the faintest cry from way up in the mountains. "I'm stuuuuuuuuuck! I'm stuck under some rooooooocks!" I heard it two nights in a row. And the night you arrived, after we played on the skateboards, I took off to find her. I went up there, up by Gorey Cliff and I got lost. And there was some talking and then a scream.

GENE. What talking? What kind of scream?

CAITLIN. A man's scream.

GENE. My father?

CAITLIN. Someone yelled something. Two syllables. It sounded something like "Weeweeeeeeee!" or "Beebeeeeeee!" And I hid behind a bush and saw the fat man. And his mouth was covered with blood, and he was talking with someone. But I can't see who. It's only a shape in the dream. I've blocked it out.

GENE. A man's shape or a women's shape?

CAITLIN. It's just a shape! And it has an ax and it chops your father in his back and he falls onto the ground. And I think he's dead already, but it chops his feet off and throws them into a ditch. And it runs away, and I faint. That's it. That's all I remember.

GENE. You're lying! You remember more. You're not telling me because you want me to suffer.

CAITLIN. No, I wouldn't —

GENE. *(Pulls out his mother's gun and points it.)* This is the gun my grandmother used to shoot herself.

CAITLIN. You can't shoot me. I'm going to St. Petersburg with

48

my lover.

GENE. Tell me what they looked like.

CAITLIN. I don't know what they looked like.

GENE. Get away from the door. *(Pause.)* Do you still see him? *(Silence.)* Do you still love Professor Raymonds?

CAITLIN. Yes.

GENE. Why? I love you and he doesn't.

CAITLIN. I don't care.

GENE. You're glad I'm like this. No legs, no dick, just baggage.

CAITLIN. Gene ...

GENE. I can't suffer enough for you. No matter how much I'm dealt.

CAITLIN. I'm sorry. Goodbye, my little Genushka. *(She pauses and then exits. Gene looks after her and then at the gun. He wheels himself to the doorway and watches Caitlin. We hear a dog barking at her ferociously. Gene holds out the gun and shoots it several times. The dog is silent. Off.)* Thanks! *(He wheels himself back in. Mrs. Slater comes running in from the apartment.)*

MRS. SLATER. Gene! What happened?! I thought you ... Give me the gun, honey. *(Takes it and puts it back in the desk.)* You don't need this. *(Goes to the window and sees the dog.)* Oh, Gene ... You ... Why did...? *(Trying to be positive.)* Well good for you, sweetheart. One less to worry about, eh , kiddo? Huh, baby?

GENE. I'm tired, Mama.

MRS. SLATER. Okay, sweetie. We'll put you down for a nap, okay?

GENE. Yeah.

MRS. SLATER. You just need to get your energy back. And after you feel better, I'll wheel you to the corner and see you off.

GENE. See me off?

MRS. SLATER. Just like I saw your daddy off. I'll be waving goodbye and you'll be on your way to the Poconos. And I'll watch until you're just a tiny speck on the horizon. And I'll come back here and settle in and think of you, out there, setting everything right. You'll set it right, Gene. You'll make everything good again. I know you will, Gene. I know you will. *(Lights fade.)*

Scene 6

Carl's van. Brad is driving at top speed, being pursued by police cars. He has been badly beaten. The sound of hundreds of sirens. Brad occasionally looks over to the invisible wallpaper devil who he sees sitting in the passenger's seat.

Scene 7

Appliance repair shop. Brad is speaking heatedly with the devil who he thinks is there. Brad is bruised, bloody and still hasn't slept in several days.

BRAD. *(To devil.)* I don't know why I listen to you! You're paper! I peeled you off a wall! *(Grabbing devil.)* I could crumple you up and no one would know you ever existed. I made you up. If you wanted — Don't interrupt me! Everything that comes out of your mouth comes out of my brain first. *(Lily enters. There is a patch of blood soaked through her shirt where the lump is.)* Well, well, well, look who's here.
LILY. What happened to you?
BRAD. I was beat up.
LILY. What?
BRAD. Things aren't good, Lily. *(Pointing at devil.)* Look. *(Lily doesn't see anything.)* Look at him! He's telling me these terrible things about you, and I don't want to believe him, but he's very persuasive! *(Turning suddenly to devil.)* Yes, I can! I can trust her! She's my friend! *(Back to Lily.)* Do you see what he's doing? He's pushing me.
LILY. Did Carl come by?
BRAD. Why didn't you tell me you were married to him?!

LILY. Who told you that?

BRAD. So it's true!

LILY. I was young at the time, just one of his students. I was lonely and stupid. I regretted it.

BRAD. You said he followed you and tried to drive you insane.

LILY. He did. I wanted to divorce him but he wouldn't let me.

BRAD. I was in love with him! I would've taken him! I never even knew he was married!

LILY. I don't know what you're talking about.

BRAD. He was here!

LILY. He was?! Did you get the tie clip?!

BRAD. No! He wants to see you over at Nelson's.

LILY. Nelson's? Where's that?

BRAD. *(Suddenly turning to devil.)* Don't tell me what to do! You've been telling me for — *(Shoved by the devil.)* Don't touch me! Get away from me!

LILY. Brad, where is Nelson's?!

BRAD. *(Being strangled by devil.)* What are you doing? I can't breathe. Stop that! *(Frees the devil's hands from around his throat and wrestles him to the ground.)* He's all right now. He just needed to let off some steam.

LILY. Brad, I have to find him! *(Rushes to the* Yellow Pages *and flips through it trying to find Nelson's.)*

BRAD. Don't be mad. It's not my fault. The devil made me do it. Know what we did? We broke into Carl's van. We were gonna gather evidence and bring it to the policewoman. And we found binoculars and a camera, and we thought now we have proof that Carl was following the boy. But then I found these photos. Photos of me! *(Throws down photos.)*

LILY. Nelson's isn't in here! This phone book is fourteen years old! *(Rushes to the phone and dials 911.)*

BRAD. Don't you see? Professor Carl Raymonds your husband, who never knew that I was in love with him, is trying to murder me because he thinks something is going on between you and me, and he never even meant to cripple that boy. He was after me the whole time.

LILY. The phone is dead! I ... oh Jesus ... I'm not feeling very well. *(Clutches her stomach in sudden pain.)* I'm gonna be sick ... I ...

(Rushes into back.)

BRAD. I didn't know what to do. So Satan taught me how to hotwire the van. My first thought was to get away, but the FDR was closed, so I drove west and took the Holland Tunnel to New Jersey, but there were cracks in it. And I thought this can't be right. I mean, the Hudson River was dribbling its way into the Holland Tunnel. And when I got out, I pulled off into a parking lot to contemplate exactly what was going on, and I could see across the river to the city, and cars were sliding off of the Westside Highway, just disappearing into the Hudson. And Satan was in the passenger's seat telling me to keep driving, to head south and forget about it, get out while I could. And I was saying something back to him, when a New York City cop tapped on the drivers side window and said "Who you talking to there, buddy boy?" And I couldn't figure out what a New York cop was doing in New Jersey, but I said, "It's Satan, officer. He floated off of my wallpaper and made me steal this van which crippled a boy." At that point I was dragged out of my vehicle and for the first time took a good look around. The parking lot was filled with New York City police cars, hundreds of them, and garbage trucks, public works vans, firetrucks, and off in the distance was a huge warehouse and there were tractor trailers pulling in shipments, handing them off to men in uniform, vats of hot coffee, crates of warm crullers. So I yelled at the cop, "What the hell is going on here?" And he started beating me with a club, and four or five other cops came waddling over and joined in, kicked me and beat me and threw donuts at my head until I couldn't move. And then they headed back to the warehouse, stuffing their bloated faces with jelly rolls. So I dragged myself to the van, started it up, and ran them down. They never had a chance. They were too fat to run. Sure, they could drag me into court, but they couldn't do anything because Satan videotaped the whole beating. *(Pulls out video. Lily throws up offstage.)* Those sons of bitches. So I ripped it out of there and started back to the city, thinking they'd never follow me, but they did. The entire NYPD leapt into their cars and followed me into the leaking tunnel, except by that time the cracks were bigger and the water was rushing in. I hydroplaned the whole way through, with hundreds of cop cars on my tail, blaring their sirens. I felt like the

Pope. Sections of tunnel were caving in behind me, water filling the place. The minute I flew up and out, the river kicked in. The Hudson came crashing down, flooding the Holland Tunnel and the entire NYPD as if the waters were the parted Red Sea falling in on the Egyptian Army, and I was Moses, safe on the other side with my people.

LILY. *(Entering, her shirt covered in blood.)* I've thrown up all this blood. I think something's wrong with me.

BRAD. And my clothes got wet. I don't like being wet, not since that sink episode. Why didn't they tell me?! My father was a garbage collector. I should know what's going on!

LILY. Brad, tell me the address to Nelson's.

BRAD. Sure, he wasn't the best garbage collector, but he was loyal. So what if his eyesight was bad? They didn't have to fire him! They could've taken him off driver duty. He didn't hit as many things as they say he did! The dogs, the children, the people with birthday cakes. They called him the Garbage Man Mauler! He didn't deserve that! *(Turns to devil.)* Stop laughing at me!

LILY. Birthday cakes?

BRAD. Why did you murder that fat man?! Why did you chop off his feet?!

LILY. I didn't!

BRAD. *(Pulling out an old bloody scarf.)* Then how do you explain this bloody scarf?

LILY. Stop stealing my things! Stay out of my room! Give that to me!

BRAD. No! I'm saving it for evidence!

LILY. Give me my scarf!

BRAD. You staggered out of the forest with one foot and a bloody stump and you never told me what happened. You flagged down my car and I drove you all the way to that hospital in St. Petersberg and you never told me what happened! You moved in here and you never told me what happened! And then I find those articles about the fat man with no feet on your sculpture and how his wife was missing a flowered silk scarf! Tell me what happened!

LILY. I want to get out of here!

CARL. *(Appears in doorway.)* Lilian, you dyed your hair. *(Lily screams and backs away from Carl. Brad runs up to him.)*

BRAD. I was in love with you, you son of a bitch! *(Wrestles Carl to the ground.)*

CARL. Get this dipshit off of me!

LILY. Give me my tie clip!

CARL. Not until you tell me what happened.

BRAD. You never paid attention to me!

CARL. I don't even know you!

BRAD. I'll kill you for saying that!

LILY. Kill the son of a bitch! *(Brad is suddenly thrown away from Carl by the invisible devil, who strangles him again.)*

CARL. What the hell's the matter with him?

LILY. Give me my tie clip!

BRAD. *(Rolling on ground with devil.)* Someone help! The devil's trying to murder me!

CARL. I thought you were dead. The fat man said you were dead.

BRAD. I wanted to leap over stuff!

LILY. Why were you taking pictures of Brad?!

BRAD. I wanted to write a children's story!

CARL. I was just watching him. That's it. *(Brad frees himself. He grabs the electric carving knife and clicks it on. He's having a standoff with the devil, waving the knife at him, while talking to Carl.)*

BRAD. I followed you everywhere, Carl, and you never noticed.

CARL. Who *are* you?

BRAD. I followed you to the Poconos. I drove behind you the whole way and you were oblivious! I lost you in the mountains! I picked up her! Your stumpy wife! I said "to hell with him!" I'll pick up this woman with one foot! I can relate. I'll visit my murderous blind father in St. Petersberg. He kept running his damn walker into me. To hell with him too! To hell with all of you! *(Runs out, the devil after him.)*

LILY. I'll never love you Carl. Accept that and give me my tie clip.

BRAD. *(Off.)* I'm borrowing your van, asshole! *(We hear the van take off with a screech.)*

CARL. I remembered you always wanted to climb Gorey Cliff.

LILY. Why did you have to find me?

CARL. So I drove to the Poconos and searched the mountains.

LILY. I didn't want to see you.

CARL. But I only found your foot.

LILY. I had an accident and had to cut it off. *(Lights also up on the laundromat. We hear the van screech to a halt outside. Mrs. Slater is closing up for the night. Brad comes running in and slams the door, just as Caitlin enters and slams the door of the fix-it shop, with a red pocketbook over her shoulder. Brad pulls down the shades and locks the door. Caitlin holds up two tickets.)*

CAITLIN. Carl, two tickets to St. Petersburg! The train leaves in three hours. I wanted to surprise you. We can get away!

CARL. Not now!

MRS. SLATER. We're closed. *(Everything freezes on stage. The lights dim. Lights up on Gene at the blackboard in front of the lecture hall. He's wearing pajamas and can walk.)*

GENE. This is a dream. I know that because I'm in my pajamas in a lecture hall filled with people and my legs work. Also, I have this Russian shell doll and I don't own one in real life. *(Shows shell doll.)* I'm not sure what I'm supposed to lecture about. I don't really know too much about anything so ... Hey, Tolstoy died in a train station. Yeah, isn't that weird? *(Writes "train station" on board.)* You know what I like about this dream? It's so quiet. Sometimes, I like to think that my dreams are my real life. And when I wake up to that laundromat, I'm really falling asleep. So, my mother isn't really my mother. She's just this lady in my dreams who says she's my mother. You know, if I reverse everything, I mean. Although, she's in both places, so ... I guess I'm stuck with her no matter what. But at least I can use my legs here. *(Lights out on him and scenes resume in laundromat and repair shop.)*

LILY. I dragged myself downhill.

BRAD. Please, my clothes are soaked.

LILY. I met a fat man who was walking cross-country to lose weight.

BRAD. *(Taking off his pants.)* There's a devil chasing me. Don't let him in here.

CAITLIN. I bought this red pocketbook for the trip.

CARL. I found your foot in the rocks.

BRAD. The devil's coming and my pants are wet.

MRS. SLATER. The dryers are busted. Now get out.

LILY. The fat man was wonderful. Like you used to be.

BRAD. I'll fix one. *(Diddles with a large dryer.)*

CAITLIN. You can't love her, Carl! She murdered Gene's father!

MRS. SLATER. *(Peeking behind shade.)* What'd you say was chasing you?

CARL. I held that foot and screamed your name!

MRS. SLATER. Is that your van out there?

CARL. Lily!

BRAD. Get away from the window! He'll find me!

CARL. Lily!

MRS. SLATER. Why is there a dent on the front of that van?

BRAD. A skateboarder was run down a few days ago. *(Crawls into the dryer to fix it.)*

CAITLIN. Carl ... That's ... that's the scream. The word in the dream.

MRS. SLATER. A skateboarder?

LILY. I heard your scream.

MRS. SLATER. You're saying innocent legs were crushed under that van?

LILY. I almost ran back to you.

MRS. SLATER. And it was your fault?

LILY. But I was strong.

BRAD. No. Someone was chasing me.

LILY. I remembered every overbearing thing you ever did to me.

BRAD. Damn, it's hot in here.

LILY. I begged the fat man.

BRAD. Can you hand me my jacket?

LILY. "Make him believe I'm never coming back." *(Mrs. Slater hands him his jacket.)*

CARL. I picked up the ax and followed the bloody trail down the mountain. *(Brad pulls the bloody scarf out of the pocket.)*

LILY. He tied a scarf around my stump to stop some of the bleeding.

BRAD. *(Wipes the sweat from his brow.)* Thanks. *(Puts scarf back.)*

LILY. He smeared some blood across his mouth and told me to go to the road. *(Mrs. Slater grabs the scarf and examines it frantically, not believing what it is. She looks at Brad in the dryer, slowly realizing.)*

CAITLIN. I had to leave Pennsylvania and come here! I hate it here!

LILY. I flagged down that damn car!

CARL. The fat man said you were gone! He said he cut you into little pieces and ate you!

LILY. You believed him?

CARL. There was blood everywhere! It looked like something he'd do.

MRS. SLATER. I wanted grandchildren.

LILY. My stomach is exploding.

CARL. He tried to run. He thought he could say something like that and get away.

MRS. SLATER. I wanted great grandchildren.

CARL. But he couldn't run for shit.

CAITLIN. You're the shape!

MRS. SLATER. I wanted a healthy family where nothing bad happened.

CAITLIN. You're the shape that whacked him in the back!

BRAD. I can't see anything wrong. Maybe we should start this thing up.

CARL. He took you away   MRS. SLATER. You took them
from me!   away from me!

CAITLIN. You chopped off his feet and threw them into a ditch! *(Lily clutches her stomach in pain, as Mrs. Slater slams the dryer shut with Brad inside.)*

LILY. There's something growling in there. Did you hear it?

BRAD. Can you wait a second?

MRS. SLATER. My cripple son can't avenge his father!

LILY. I have to get out of here!

CAITLIN. My dreams are your fault! *(Carl goes to the door to block Lily's way.)*

BRAD. Could you
open the door?!   LILY. Open the door!

CAITLIN. *(Pulling at Carl.)* I was six years old and you ruined me!

MRS. SLATER. I thought this cancer could be removed!

CARL. *(Throwing Caitlin across the room.)* Get the fuck off me!

MRS. SLATER. But it can't.

LILY. *(Grabs electric knife.)* Give me my tie clip!

MRS. SLATER. There's always a little piece of it that flares up and comes out again.

CARL. *(Grabbing train tickets.)* Come to St. Petersburg.

57

MRS. SLATER. *(Popping quarters into dryer.)* He was a wonderful fat man and you cut him down!

LILY. *(Takes tickets from him.)* I want to leave by myself!

BRAD. I had nothing to do with that! *(Lily throws open the door to the fix-it shop just as the door to the laundromat flies open and the wallpaper devil enters. Things are knocked over as the devil approaches the dryer. Carl grabs Lily so she can't leave.)*

LILY. Let go of me! *(The dryer door flies open.)*

BRAD. Don't let him in here! No! *(Lily slices knife across Carl's ankle. Carl screams as Brad screams. Mrs. Slater slams the dryer door closed and turns it on.)*

CARL. Goddamit! *(Lily runs out of the fix-it shop as Brad is tumble-dried to death. Carl limps out after her. Caitlin is on ground, crying.)*

CAITLIN. St. Petersburg ... St. Petersburg ... *(Lights fade on fix-it shop. Carl appears in the doorway to the laundromat, shaking.)*

CARL. Where is my wife!

MRS. SLATER. We're closed!

CARL. That van out front! Did she duck in here?

MRS. SLATER. That's a shiny tie clip you have.

CARL. That's a big belt you're wearing.

MRS. SLATER. *(Grabs tie clip.)* I know someone who's looking for a tie clip that fits that description.

CARL. *(Grabs the belt.)* I've only seen a belt like that on a fat man who couldn't run well.

MRS. SLATER. What did you say?

CARL. This clip used to belong to my wife. I found it in the Poconos when I killed a fat man who I thought ate her. But he didn't eat her. She's alive. Have you seen the man with the devil? Maybe they're together. He stole my van. That's my van. Are they in here? Are they hiding in here?

MRS. SLATER. That's your van? *(Pulls away from him.)*

CARL. Give me my tie clip.

MRS. SLATER. *(Pulls out the gun.)* This is the gun my mother used to shoot herself. *(She shoots him. He falls to the ground.)*

CARL. Oh, God ...

MRS. SLATER. They were babies, innocent babies.

CARL. *(Noticing baby blanket piece on her sweater.)* Where did you get that baby blanket?

MRS. SLATER. That's none of your business.

CARL. Do you know me? *(Pulls out matching piece of baby blanket.)* This is all that I have of where I came from.

MRS. SLATER. *(Looking at blanket.)* That's my baby brother's ... but you ... *(Pause.)* You killed my husband. You crippled my boy.

CARL. I was found in an alley, wrenched out of a dog's mouth.

MRS. SLATER. Cracker ate you.

CARL. Cracker? *(He picks up the gun on the floor and looks at it.)* Mommy shot herself?

MRS. SLATER. Because you were gone.

CARL. Because of me?

MRS. SLATER. I'm sorry, Dmitry.

CARL. Dmitry? My name is Dmitry? *(He dies. She looks down at her brother and then over at the dryer. She goes to the dryer and opens it. Brad's body falls out halfway, his skin is red and burned.)*

MRS. SLATER. An innocent man ... *(She slowly and deliberately takes off the belt across her chest as the lights fade.)*

Scene 8

Lights up on Lily and Caitlin, who see each other across a train platform. We hear a loud train approach. Caitlin has her red bag. Lily has the train tickets.

CAITLIN. Hey! Carl is in the laundromat!

LILY. I'm going to St. Petersburg! *(Holds up the tickets.)*

CAITLIN. You have to go back!

LILY. What?

CAITLIN. Laundromat!

LILY. I can't hear you!

CAITLIN. Go back and tell him what I've done! *(The sound of the train is deafening. There's a loud whistle and Caitlin throws herself in front of the train. Blackout.)*

Scene 9

Lights up in the laundromat. Brad's body is still hanging out of the dryer. Carl is dead on the floor. Mrs. Slater has hung herself with her husband's belt. We can see the bottom of her feet swinging from above. Gene is in the middle of it all with his giant backpack strapped to the back of his wheelchair. He's blowing up a life raft. He has the jar with the one foot in it on his lap. Lily limps in, carrying a bloody laundry bag with something in it. She can barely stand. Water may be flooding the store.

LILY. I missed my train. Your friend ... I saved this for her parents. *(Puts bag down.)*

GENE. I'm leaving.

LILY. *(Takes in laundromat.)* What ... happened here?

GENE. I don't know. I took a nap upstairs. I had the most wonderful dream and came down to this.

LILY. *(Notices Carl.)* Carl ... Carl? *(Drags herself to him and searches him.)*

GENE. I'm gonna take this raft to the Poconos and knock on every door along the way and show them this. *(Refers to foot in jar.)* My glass slipper. I'm going to find out who murdered my father.

LILY. I can't find my clip.

GENE. My mother hung herself.

LILY. *(Looks up at Mrs. Slater sadly.)* Ohhh. *(Sees tie clip on her.)* Oh! Oh, look! She got it! She got it for me! My tie clip! Up there! See how shiny it is?! *(Lying on the ground, too weak to move.)*

GENE. I'll find the killer. I'll do it for my mother.

LILY. Help me, Gene. Help me get it down.

GENE. I've got his maps. And this foot.

LILY. Please, Gene. I can't ... *(Sudden pain in her stomach.)* Oh God. Did you hear a bark in there? Something is chewing its way out and barking at me. *(Rests her head on Carl's chest.)* Gene, if you

60

get me my clip, I'll tell you something.

GENE. I gotta go.

LILY. No, I'll tell you. Just get me my ...

GENE. Look after the store for me.

LILY. *(Weakly.)* We have to talk.

GENE. No more talk. *(Wheels himself to the door.)*

LILY. Your father ...

GENE. Wish me luck!

LILY. Wait, Gene ...

GENE. I'm going to the Poconos!

LILY. Gene ...

GENE. I'll avenge him!

LILY. Ge ...

GENE. Avenge my footless father! *(Lily dies. Gene pushes himself off, the giant backpack strapped to his wheelchair. Lights fade.)*

End of Play

PROPERTY LIST

Telephone
Homemade "Happy Birthday" banner (MRS. SLATER)
Plaid shirt (GENE)
Flyers (MRS. SLATER)
Socks (GENE)
Photos (MRS. SLATER, CAITLIN, BRAD)
Boots (GENE)
Book (CAITLIN)
Electric carving knife (BRAD, LILY)
Pencil, sketch pad (LILY)
Compass (MRS. SLATER)
Pen, journal (CARL)
Gift-wrapped present of jar containing two feet in
    formaldehyde (MRS. SLATER)
Jar containing one foot in formaldehyde (MRS. SLATER)
Backpack (MRS. SLATER)
Ring (MRS. SLATER)
Skateboard (GENE, MRS. SLATER, BRAD)
Sewing materials, rain slicker (MRS. SLATER)
Quarters (MRS. SLATER)
Huge pair of shoes (MRS. SLATER)
Maps and brochures (MRS. SLATER)
Cigarettes, matches (CARL, CAITLIN)
Napkins (CARL)
Bag from Radio Shack (BRAD)
Prosthetic foot (BRAD)
Ceramic foot with newspaper articles pasted on it (BRAD)
Old, flowered, silk scarf stained with blood (BRAD)
Gun (CARL)
Binoculars, camera (CAITLIN)
Dostoyevsky's Nightmares (LILY)
Protein bar (LILY)
Bandage (BRAD)
Bag of ice (BRAD)
Stack of dusty old books (BRAD)
Wheelchair (GENE)

Dinner plate with food, utensils (MRS. SLATER)
Revolver (MRS. SLATER, GENE)
Steak knife (GENE)
Papers (CARL)
Eyepatch (BRAD)
Envelope (LILY)
Videotape (BRAD)
Red pocketbook (CAITLIN)
Two tickets (CAITLIN)
Chalk (GENE)
Russian shell doll (GENE)
Jacket (MRS. SLATER)
Life raft (GENE)
Bloody laundry bag (LILY)
Tie clip (LILY)

SOUND EFFECTS

Washers and dryers running
Dogs barking
Dogs chasing someone
Dogs devouring food
Subway
Phone ringing
Carl's voice-over
Metal grates being lifted
Gunshots
Police sirens
Screech of van
Approaching train
Train whistle